These memories of mothers have all been written by YOURS readers

Dedicated to our mums and yours - the YOURS team

A LOVE OF LIFE

'She sparkled with happiness - encouraging, supporting, not only her own family but other village families as well'

M Y MOTHER died last year. She was ninety. She had lived all her life in the small mining village of Silkstone in the old West Riding of Yorkshire. The village was her life, her strength, and her joy.

Throughout her life, which was hard, she never lost her love of life. She sparkled with happiness - encouraging, supporting, not only her own family but other village families too.

My mother and father were born and brought up doors away from each other in Silkstone. On school photographs dad, a year older than mum, is standing behind her, his hand on her shoulder.

They married in May 1925, a sad day as mother's father died a week before the wedding date and instead of a truly village occasion only the family attended the quiet service at eight o'clock in the morning.

The photograph which Emma gave to her children before she died

"No celebrations," Mum told me many years later. "After breakfast of bacon and tomatoes your dad and me went for a walk round the village where all our friends came out to wish us happiness."

A sad start, but worse was to come. A year later, and three months pregnant with me, my father had a serious illness. A TB spine was diagnosed and for six months he was in hospital. Returning home, for another six months he had to lie flat on his back waiting patiently for his back to get stronger.

It was 1926, the year of the General Strike. The small terraced house must have been bulging at the seams as the whole family coped. Dad on his sick bed, a new baby, my mother, grandparents, and an aunt and uncle all trying to make ends meet. Mum was allowed eight shillings a week for herself and the baby, but the family couldn't manage, and grandma insisted that grandad break the strike and go back to work. The village mining community never forgave him.

"But I was young," mother used to tell me, "and in spite of all our hardships we had lots of laughs. The parson loaned dad one of the first wireless sets, and he was never short of a mate to listen in with him. And we were so busy washing, ironing and baking all our own bread, that we didn't have time to feel sorry for ourselves. There was always someone ready to lend a hand, we had plenty of advisers and counsellors here in the village."

Father recovered, things got better, and mum had her own house in the village. We were always hard up, but my brother and I never knew it.

Mum was a marvellous manager; there was a tin for everything. The Christmas tin, the Blackpool tin (yes we always had a week at Blackpool). In 1936, dad said, he took five pounds with him and it covered all expenses.

There was a clothes tin - mum would never let us go without a new outfit at Whitsuntide. There were also the usual bill tins - doctors, insurance and food.

We never missed Sunday dinner of roast beef and Yorkshire pudding; even to this day my Yorkshire puddings aren't a patch on what mum's were.

Left a widow in 1968, once again mum found comfort and

strength in her village. During the 25 years she lived alone mum had four break-ins. I pleaded with her to come and live with me, but no, she said, "They're not getting me to leave Silkstone that easily".

A few years before she died mum presented all her family with a photograph of herself as a young girl of seventeen taken while on holiday at Blackpool. We never knew her like this, but mother wanted us to see her young, eager, beautiful as she was.

"My hair was long and red," she said, "I could sit on it. The photograph was coloured and enlarged and put on show in the window at Blackpool. Folks came back and told me they'd seen it."

Emma and her husband in 1926. Father was learning to walk again after his illness

The church was full at my mother's funeral. Young and old from the village came to say farewell to the old lady who had lived there all her life. As someone said to me, "It'll never be the same again in Silkstone without Emma Mellor."

I smiled as I realised this was her maiden name, the name the village had always known her by. Mum would have liked that.

Isabel Hughes, Southwell

A WOMAN OF MANY PARTS

'Friends rallied round to help that valiant woman rebuild our lives. Never once did she cry, at least before us'

MY MOTHER was a tiny lady with fair skin, blue/grey eyes, and beautiful auburn hair which - when unbraided - stretched well beyond her waist. It was a joy for us children to take turns brushing it.

She was a loving, gentle, deeply religious person, who could on occasion be absolutely resolute when she thought something we were requesting was not good for us. But when she said the magic words "I'll see what your father thinks," we knew she had already decided in our favour, but would put it to him in such a way, he thought *he* was deciding.

She had a wonderful sense of humour and a fund of funny stories. Her God - the God of Love - was within her, a god to whom she often turned in supplication, in thanks. I think this was the secret of her happiness - her contentment and acceptance of life.

God was a part of our growing up, a loving friend, to whom we were taught to pray, rather than say prayers. We were taught the tenets of our faith before we went to school, not as 'do's and don'ts', but as a means of strengthening our faith in, and love for, Him. After bathing each night, we sat round the fire to pray together and sing hymns before cocoa and bed.

What I remember most about her was she was always there singing as she knitted, sewed, cooked, or cleaned. She taught us politeness, respect, kindness, honesty, forgiveness, loyalty, and instilled into us a deep sense of 'togetherness'. We often played card games or if spirits were low had an impromptu concert.

Tale-bearing was discouraged. Two maxims come to mind - "A rumour has sent many a good man to the gallows," and, "Never do anything of which you know I would be ashamed".

She taught us to be generous to the less fortunate, the elderly, foreign missionaries and the poor.

For misdemeanours we were deprived of privileges - Sunday matinee, dessert or cake, or sweets, but we were never slapped.

To bring up six children in Ireland in the 1930s on a naval man's salary called for a careful and thrifty manager, and Mamma was all that. She made, mended, refashioned, knitted, crocheted, paying a bi-annual visit to the local woollen mills to buy remnants or flawed material during the 'Sales'. Shoes were mended by my father when on shore leave.

Meals were plain and wholesome and not very expensive as there were no middle men. Flour was bought from the mill, homemade butter from the milkman. Bacon and sausages and black pudding were cheap. We only had meat twice weekly, for fish was plentiful and cheap.

When the boys went hunting a welcome rabbit found its way into the pot. A large marrow bone was always included in the meat order, which with fresh vegetables made delicious soup. Dessert was served on Sundays only.

School uniforms and books were some of the costliest items of the year. Uniforms were passed down or on, depending on the current finances. Mamma encouraged us to keep our books neat and clean; these we sold at half price at the end of term. Every weekend we each had to clean our uniforms with petrol, then damp-press them in readiness for Monday following.

Disaster struck in the summer of 1936 - we grew up overnight. Fire destroyed our home, leaving us with only the clothes we were wearing. Every trace of our early life together was reduced to a pile of smoking ash on a rectangle of concrete foundation.

Over the next few weeks friends rallied round to help that valiant woman rebuild our lives. Never once did she cry, at least before us.

She set to, sorting out the oddments of furniture so generously donated by our friends. Gone forever were the photographs, mementoes, the little sentimental things of no financial value but of priceless worth. The love which these symbolised remained steadfast.

As we grew older, we found Mamma was a woman of many parts. She was the family psychiatrist and counsellor, the confidant of teenage secrets and tragedies, the judge and arbitrator, the accountant and banker, the doctor and nurse, but never the patient.

In 1939 my eldest sister left home to become a nun, followed two years later by myself. Mamma was honoured that God had chosen two daughters to serve in his household. She gave us generously, but no-one saw the heartbreak, so well did she hide her hurts.

Because of the war. I did not see her until 1948, as visas were difficult to obtain. The monthly letters kept the bond of love strong.

In the early Fifties she sold up in Ireland and moved to England to "be near my children". Her grandchildren were her delight, in fact she was 'Nanna' to every child in the street.

In 1980 she fell, broke her femur and pneumonia followed. From December 13th to the 27th she lay in pain, never complaining. We never left her. She could say on her death bed when asked if she was ready for Heaven, "I don't know, but I do know that I have never designedly hurt anyone. I have tried to be kind to everyone I met, not that it was always accepted, but that did not prevent me from offering at another time". She died as she lived, gently, tranquilly, fully aware of each of us.

Sister Julia E Conneely

PHIL SILVERS remembers his 'momma' as plump and short. He says is wasn't until he was old enough to appreciate women's looks that he realised she was very pretty. Although she grew up in America, evidently her vision of life was one she'd brought over from Russia. This was, said Phil - love your children, keep them warm and well-fed - and never trust a friendly Gentile!

THE FAMILY COMES FIRST

'I was an only child, but never spoilt'

I HAD a very happy childhood. I was an only child, but never spoilt. My parents encouraged me to be self-reliant and to join organisations like Brownies, Girl Guides, Junior Red Cross.

They were far from rich, but I was taken on seaside and farm holidays until the war put an end to all that.

During the war mum queued up for food, gathered wood from building sites, looked after my grandfather when he came to live with us, had a family to stay each summer to give them a rest from the bombs, plus various soldiers and airmen who were billetted on us. She was also forced to go out to work in an office two days a week - by Government order.

Now, if I'm on my own and feel like grumbling about my arthritis, I remember my mum who never complained, and feel very humble.

Patricia Jackson, Leeds

'A Londoner at heart'

MY MOTHER came from a comfortable, though not well off, family - a Londoner by upbringing and at heart. She married, in her late thirties, my deaf father. He soon became unemployed and she found herself moved to various uncomfortable country homes managing on the dole - 10/- for a man, 5/- for her and 2/6 for me.

She was determined I should speak nicely, go to a nice school and look good. When I got a scholarship to a girls' public school at a younger age than most, she did her utmost to keep me there.

My father was as well cared for as I was and it was he who I loved. It wasn't until I was much older that I appreciated her - the court dressmaker from London transplanted to the heart of rural Bedfordshire - determined that her one child should have all life's benefits.

DM, Much Wenlock

(reader asks to be anonymous)

MUSICAL MUMS

'She put on Dad's suit and sang and acted'

SHE had eleven of us, and my dad was very hard on us. He was an ex-army sergeant and treated us like soldiers. If we read a book we were breeding fleas, if our bodice or shoulder strap slipped from under our sleeve he would cut it - it was all spit and polish.

But when he went out my mum was lovely. She'd sing and dance to us and dress up. Our favourite was when she put on dad's suit and sang and acted Burlington Bertie. What a rush to get them off if he came back too soon.

Grace Maynard, Forest Gate

'Making toast while she belted out a stanza or two'

I ALWAYS thought the fact that she had Welsh blood must account for her great love of music. My earliest memory is of mum kneeling by the open fire making toast while she belted out a stanza or two from The Merry Widow. As soon as I was old enough I joined in.

Together we roamed back and forth with equal facility between Dolly Gray and the symphonies of Beethoven. It always grieved mum that she and dad could never afford a piano, or for that matter, rooms large enough to house one.

She could play a little and would give us The Maiden's Prayer, or perhaps The Robin's Return, when we visited luckier friends with a piano.

She is not forgotten, never could be while there's music. This is, in a way, I suppose, just about the best memorial that anyone could have.

Dorothy Gubbins, Carshalton

'When there was a storm we would all sing until it was over'

MY MOTHER was a lady, and a very genteel person, with lots of patience - which she needed to contend with her large family of five sons and five daughters.

She taught us all to knit, even the boys, and often on a cold wet winter's day we would come home from school to find wool and a pair of needles for each of us. We would all sit round the cosy fire and knit until teatime.

When there was a storm she would usher us all into the parlour, play the piano and we would all sing until it was over.

My mother's favourite hymn was Rock of Ages and if we beat her in an argument she used to sing it. We all joined in so by the time we finished no one knew what the argument was about.

She never went to bed until we were all tucked up and asleep. Then she would go with her clock, purse and a plate with a slice of bread and butter on it. She ate this sometime in the night, the only time, she said, when she had the peace and quiet to enjoy it!

We all have very fond memories of her and always will.

Edith Maud Wicker, Basildon

'She sang as she kneaded bread'

MY MOTHER was beautiful, but what I remember most about her was her singing. She sang as she rocked us to sleep, she sang as she kneaded bread, black-leaded the fireplace, polished the brass, scrubbed the floors - whatever she was doing, she sang as she did it. And she was always there.

Because of her happy singing we all learned dozens of the old songs. Because of her I sang to my children, and they sing to theirs.

She has been dead 25 years but I remember her every day when I find myself humming or singing one of the songs she sang to us.

Sheila Hindley, Workington

'We had hummed Carmen and Swan Lake'

MUM HAD a love of music as she had been a lady's maid/companion to the first Lady Beecham so, instead of lullabies, we had hummed Carmen and Swan Lake!

Later, living in a cottage on the country estate of Lady Beecham, mum learned to make pegged rugs and sometimes sold one for real money (usually our village dealt in barter - "A piglet, OK?").

The main rule in our house was tell the truth. The slightest deviation from this caused us to be punished without exception.

Elsie Walker, Weston-Super-Mare

'A real virago all five feet nothing'

THE CUDDLES were carried out by dad; he couldn't bear to see any of the 12 of us upset. So it was Fan (as everyone called my mother), a real virago all five-foot-nothing of commonsense, thrift and fairness, that ruled the nest.

She was a marvellous cook, as Worple Road and Swaffield Road wartime firemen will vouch for!

She had a wonderful sense of humour. At parties she and her friend Sue Brown would bring things to an end with their rendering of Who's Taking Me Home Tonight. As most of the parties were at our house, and Sue lived round the corner, there were no takers!

Constance Mellish, Earlsfield

11

THINGS MOTHER TAUGHT ME

'She encouraged me to get on with life'

M Y FATHER walked out on my mother and me soon after this picture (below) was taken in 1937. I was just six months old.

We lived with my mother's mother, who was already well into her seventies. It must have been a desperate time for my mother keeping three of us on my grandmother's pension and the 10 shillings a week which my father paid for my maintenance. How

Wilma's daughters Heloise and Alele
and her grandchildren Lewis and Sorrel

skilfully she must have managed.

I was taught to work hard, be honest and think of others. I was encouraged to sit the 11-plus exam which gave me a place at the grammar school. I went on to college and obtained my degree.

My mother gave me the greatest gift of all - the encouragement to get on with life.

I have tried to do the same for my daughters. I was widowed in 1974 when the girls were just 14 and 6. I've tried to give them the same love, security and encouragement, together with a sense of self-worth.

Wilma Gravenor, Taunton

'The smell of the rag and bone merchants is still well remembered'

I AM the youngest of a family of 17 children. My mother was just 21 when she met my father, who was a widower left with 11 children, all still at home.

She worked very hard to care for us all. I never saw my dear mum idle; she was always working, even on a Sunday she would be making and mending.

I can still recall plainly the values she instilled in us all to always speak the truth and only speak when you're spoken to.

Cleanliness was the first in the order set for us all, and patching and darning everything (talk about make do and mend - that was our natural way of life!).

My brother and I always had to take the clean, worn-out woollies (patches as well), plus the worn-out cottons, to the local rag and bone merchants. Gosh, the smell is still well remembered! We got it weighed and then queued at the foreman's office and got maybe as much as 2/6 for it. It was a small fortune to take back to mother.

We were taught to be honest, clean and care about others.

Every day she always changed from her working dress and wrap-over overall into a different dress and pinafore for the afternoons and evening.

Joyce Clutsom, Bristol

'It was obvious that my mother was the best of all'

ON MOTHERING Sunday in the 1920s we would sing a chorus which went like this:

My mother's the best of all,
She watches and tends me all the time
And helps me up when I fall.
My mother's the best of all;
And when she's old and worn and grey,
She'll still be the best of all.

14

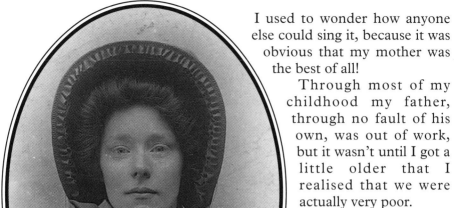

I used to wonder how anyone else could sing it, because it was obvious that my mother was the best of all!

Through most of my childhood my father, through no fault of his own, was out of work, but it wasn't until I got a little older that I realised that we were actually very poor.

One day when my mother had been feeding a tramp in our kitchen I said, "You can't afford to give food away to a tramp!".

She then taught me a lesson I have never forgotten. She just said: "God is no man's debtor, what we give He always repays and He giveth and giveth and giveth again".

I have found through the years the truth of that statement - so thank you to the best mother in the world for that and many other lessons you taught me.

Winifred Backhouse, Benfleet

'Time to listen costs nothing'

A SMILE, kindness and time to listen costs nothing, but can make a great deal of difference to someone with troubles - this was something our mother always told us.

We had a harmonium and some afternoons she and her friends - all of them with young children and very little money - would get together and sing. I can always picture them when I hear 'Jerusalem'.

Joyce Dunster, Cambridge

'We always said our prayers at bedtime'

M Y DEAR mother brought us up to respect others. We always said grace before and after meals and our prayers at bedtime.

Most important of all, if we were ever in difficulties or ill she told us to turn round and face it, never to put off difficult situations.

Mrs Guess, Clevedon

CARE AND COMFORT

'I hid the nasty bits of my dinner in the pockets of my knickers'

MOTHER taught me to take care while crossing the road at a dangerous corner. I was also told to always keep my hands around the brake levers of my bicycle, in readiness for an emergency stop.

One should never sit on public toilet seats, for fear of infection - this advice I, too, gave to my children, who even though adults now, still practise it!

Of course, there were the usual platitudes: 'Mind your Ps and Qs,' 'Speak when you are spoken to,' and, 'Little girls should be seen and not heard'.

One had to take the nearest cake when at the table and I was only allowed the one. I still shudder at the memories of kissing the visiting aunts good-night.

When we were in bed in the evening, I can remember mother sewing on her treadle machine. She would be repairing sheets, 'sides to middle', as she called it.

The button tin was a wonderful thing to delve into, when I was bored and especially when ill and confined to bed. I was also allowed, as a special treat, mother's jewellery box, which would be a fancy chocolate box full of glass beads and colourful bangles.

Mother was patient and comforting when I was ill. She would tell me tales of how the stork brought me, and about Father Christmas, convincing me of their authenticity.

There would be a coal fire lit, not only for warmth but to cheer me up too, and mother would even sleep with me sometimes at night, offering me such delicacies as her homemade barley water, which soothed a sore throat beautifully.

Even in those far-off, safe days, mother warned me of the dangers of speaking to strangers and to never accept gifts of money or sweets or lifts in cars.

Hazel and puppy Barry

I was taught never to owe anybody money - 'Only buy what you can afford'. Mother would have various compartments in her tin cash box, all labelled clearly as to whom she had to pay money to.

The thing that made mother cross was when I hid the nasty bits of my dinner in the pocket of my knickers (otherwise I would have been forced to sit at the table till teatime until the plate was clean).

Mother got cross when I told an aristocratic old lady that she often bought my clothes from jumble sales: we might have been poor, but we didn't have to stoop so low as to accept charity!

We were taught never to go out with torn or soiled socks and underwear, just in case we should have an accident.

The shame of somebody finding us in such a state would not bear contemplating!

Hazel Rawlings, Crowborough

CHARACTERS IN THEIR OWN RIGHT

'She quite fancied herself as a carpenter'

MY MOTHER was a naval wife in the late 20s, 30s and, thanks to the Second World War, into the mid-50s. A slim, pretty woman, she ruled me with a rod of iron, or more usually the business side of a hair brush.

In those far off days, sea-going naval men were given tours of duty lasting three years. My father was nearly always sent to the China station. He must have been more familiar with Shanghai than with his own home town. My sister and I hardly knew this handsome, benevolent man.

Our stalwart mother was the parent we always turned to with our childish problems, real or imaginary, and she was always there.

She was a resourceful woman and would attempt any repairs if she thought she had half a chance of being successful.

On one very memorable occasion she changed a fuse after a light bulb failed. Upon pushing the switch down, a huge blue flame shot across the room from the direction of the fuse box.

The three of us rushed to the back door and ran the length of the garden path to stand panting at the gate, only venturing back indoors when all seemed quiet.

My mother's repairs resulted in our house being without electricity for 48 hours.

She quite fancied herself as a carpenter. Using a ruler to measure before sawing was tedious and irksome. Instead, she relied on her good eyesight. The result was that three chairs and the kitchen table each had one leg standing on a wad of paper or a cigarette packet to stop them wobbling.

In good weather she was an enthusiastic walker, dragging her two daughters and Bill the dog with her.

My mother's worries must have been many and various. My

sister's constant illnesses and my thoughtless, adventurous spirit must have caused her many sleepless nights. The war also took its toll.

Through the years mother's dry sense of humour and her fun have kept the family on an even keel.

Two years ago this grand lady died at the age of 87, still arguing and trying to put the world to rights. And oh, how we miss her.

Jacqueline Richardson, Kirkcaldy

'She made me a lovely golliwog from an old black wool stocking'

MY MUM was only 4 foot 10 inches, very tiny, like Barbara Windsor. My dad made her a high wooden stool so she could sit and sew and get near the light. Sewing was how she stretched out her meagre wages.

We all had to take our turn helping. To make things more fair she wrote down all the jobs to be done for the week on pieces of paper, folded them up and put them in the pink sugar bowl. Whatever jobs we picked out we had to do for that week.

Her old hand sewing machine never stopped and she used up everything.

One year she made me a lovely gollywog from an old black wool stocking with lovely big pearl buttons for his eyes.

My father backed her up all the way. Of course they had the odd row, but it didn't last long; it was mostly over money and my poor old dad having a pint now and again.

Olive Clyne, Ruislip

'She put an emerald green feather on her hat'

WE WENT from London to Swansea when I was two years old. My mother had to cope with Welsh-speaking friends, neighbours and tradesmen.

Her clothes were different as she did not wear a shawl. Instead she wore a big purple coat. The villagers had no part in Votes for Women and did not know that Liberty's of Regent Street dyed the cloth so that the group would recognise each other.

My mother was the middle of three daughters. The eldest wanted to be a teacher but as their father died when he was 44, that became impossible so she was apprenticed to a printers and did black bordering by hand for the Royal household.

The youngest girl had more money spent on her and learnt to play the violin. Relations bought her a little harmonium so she could play hymns on Sunday.

My mother was taken on as a companion to a rich aunt with two boys in Ilford. She caused a great stir when she got tired of having to wear black because Queen Victoria was dead and put an emerald green feather on her hat!

She had a good home and a better life than the other girls but missed their love and company. She used to spend her pocket money on them when she joined them for a birthday party or special Sunday lunch.

Because my father's wages were higher in Wales than in London, my mother thought she should possess a piano. She chose one, an upright grand in walnut, with brass candlesticks.

The newel post and three stairs had to be taken down to enable the men to get it into the back parlour. It would not stand square and straight as one of the castors had gone through a floorboard.

She was never willing to play for the second verse of a hymn, so we had to sing the rest.

She lived to be 84 and was quite happy not being a pianist.

Wyn Lawrence

'Had Old Nick appeared in front of her she would have sent him packing'

I OFFER heartfelt thanks to my mother for giving me the ability to mix with every type and character of person, so that I can walk into a room and mingle at once, adapting and feeling fully confident.

I was an only child and she was determined that I stand on my own feet. In some ways she was hard, but it has certainly paid dividends for I've been able to stand up to the slings and arrows of life.

She firmly believed that 'as ye sow, so shall ye reap' and this was drummed into my ears non stop each day.

I have never met anyone as fearless as she. Nobody scared her, nor any situation. Had Old Nick appeared in front of her she would have sent him packing.

She was not a sentimental mother. There were no cuddles if I fell over, and if bullied by anyone I was sent to sort it out myself. But, by golly, it paid off as, like her, I can also take on anyone.

Physically she was strong too, with contempt for folk 'who ran to the doctor if their little finger ached', as she put it.

A dyed-in-the-wool country woman, she cured herself with herbs, lived until 91 with all her faculties intact, and never used a washing machine or a telephone.

Eileen Glover, Richmond, Surrey

'In her heyday my mum was a little wow'

DURING her late Forties my mother took badly to a miscarriage, the ensuing menopause and the lack of money. Without money her life was utterly miserable.

She and my dad had known what it was to be big spenders, but at a time when so many men were being thrown out of a job, things went from bad to awful!

Once she bought secondhand gas cookers intending to do them up for resale, at another time it was clocks.

Not for many years did my father know where the money came from, until he looked for his best suit and found it was at the pawnbrokers.

The irony was that when she came away with the money raised from pledging her silverware and many of her lovely rings, she'd fill the house with flowers.

Reconditioning prams and washing dogs were two later enthusiasms.

Retired proprietors of a Plymouth hotel, my mum and dad lived into their mid 80s. Mum was finally taken to hospital where she spent the rest of her days and became known as The Duchess because she kept everybody on their toes.

When the matron tinkled a bell to inform visitors that it was time to leave, mum, humorous to the end, was known to shout to the ward in general: "Time, gentlemen, please".

A character in her own right, in her heyday my mum was a little wow!

Nina Kenworthy, Liverpool

23

A LOVING HEART

'She would give up her last sixpence, being generous to a fault'

MY MOTHER and her five brothers and four sisters all lived with their parents in a tiny two-up and two-down in south east London.

Their parents drank heavily and were never in a fit state to care for the children. It fell on my mother's shoulders to look after them and to try to feed them with what money was left after most of it was spent on beer.

In those days - early 1900s - bread was sold by weight. When mother went into the baker's shop to get a cottage loaf the baker would put the bread on the scale and add a small piece that was called a make-weight. She was so hungry that she would eat this extra piece before she returned home, although she knew she would get a beating for doing so.

On her fourteenth birthday she left school and worked first in a sweet factory and then a corset factory. Next she went into service, where she was ill-treated. After her mistress had gone to bed one night she crept downstairs, knocking over a big hallstand as she did so, and fled leaving the street door wide open.

During the First World War she was a fore-lady in a sausage factory working on a machine that filled the sausagemeat into the skins.

She met my father while he was home on leave from the army and they married when she was 18 and he 20 years old.

I feel that because she was deprived of any kind of love and affection in her young life, her own heart was full of love for others. She would walk miles to help anyone in need, having no money for tram fairs. Indeed she would give up her last sixpence, being generous to a fault.

I grew up in a home full of love.

My father found it difficult to find work after the war and we lived in a single room where mum had a gas ring in the hearth on which she had to do her cooking.

I never felt that I lacked anything as I was always dressed in neat and tidy clothes, even a school uniform when I passed the scholarship and went to a Central School near the Elephant and Castle.

She taught me to be well-mannered and considerate to other people and to speak when spoken to and not butt in.

"You are a phenomenon." These were the words spoken to my mother by her doctor when she was in her 93rd year. He was right. She was a very special lady.

Elsie Nicholls, Maidstone

LOVELY PEOPLE

'Mum and I used to dig the whole of the back garden'

OUR MOTHER was one of the best cooks and dressmakers there was. She made marvellous meals out of a small piece of meat with plenty of vegetables and suet dumplings. This helped to fill up three growing girls.

She brought us up on her own as dad was in the navy and away for long periods.

During the war mum and I used to dig the whole of the back garden and plant it with vegetables.

She used to go to secondhand shops - where no clothing coupons were required - and buy ladies' coats and dresses. She washed and unpicked them and made us lovely clothes.

It could not have been easy for mother, not having dad there to support and help her. But like thousands of other wives and mothers she carried on and looked after the house and her children.

We all loved our mum. She was simply the best.

Mrs Verrall, Havant

'We played at mothers and fathers and our mother had a well-deserved rest'

AT 27 my mother was left a widow with four children under eight. I remember every Good Friday she would buy a bag of hot cross buns, take bottles of water (no canned drinks in those days) and the family would walk across the fields to some woods nearby.

Here was a sheltered place called The Warren where primroses, violets and anemones grew in abundance. We children played at mothers and fathers and our mother had a well-deserved rest.

During the war she was befriended by the wife of a hotel manager and was given a job serving behind the bar. There she met my stepfather who was a regular soldier in the Royal Engineers. He must have loved her a great deal as, in spite of we four children, they were married.

Three generations - Margaret, her daughter and her mother

He really was a super man and cared for us as if we were his own children. Never having known a father it was wonderful to be able to speak of 'my daddy' to the other girls at school.

Being brought up by my mother to watch the pennies I have never been in debt. I would go without near essentials rather than owe money to anyone.

She taught me to use my initiative and I aways tried to better myself, ending up with a good position in the civil service.

My mother certainly made an impact on my life. Although she died some 20 years ago, I often think of her and talk of her to my daughters.

Margaret Rixon, Twyford

Margaret's older brother and mother

'There were lots of sheds so she could have the animals she had always liked'

ELSIE MAY, my mother, was brought up on a farm in the heart of Lincolnshire by foster parents who later adopted her. In her teens she went into service to a big house in London where she met and married my father.

When five children came into her life she was very pleased, loved the company, being an only child herself.

During the war she was advised to take us off to the country. Dad stayed and looked after the house. She looked after us very well on her own.

When dad died she started looking for a mate. It wasn't long before she married again and had four more mouths to feed.

Mother's new husband took us to a house in a pretty village.

There were lots of sheds so she could have the animals she had always liked - pigs, bantams, ducks, chickens, rabbits, a cat and a dog.

She loved the flowers she grew in her garden and picked bunches of them which she got us to give to neighbours.

She loved her radio programmes - Edmundo Ros and Valentine Dyall as The Man in Black.

When we were all safely asleep in bed mother and dad often on moonlight nights took a walk around the village, arm in arm, listening to the sounds.

She was a very contented mother.

Yvonne Godfrey, Witney

'What can't be cured must be endured'

MY MOTHER was born in May 1888 and was 'put into service' at the age of 12 as a day maid for a local well-off family.

She met my father when he was a soldier in Hillsborough Barracks. They married in 1909 and had five children. Two died in infancy. We - the surviving three - are still creaking along.

My father was severely shell-shocked in the First World War. His injuries affected him severely and he walked out on us in 1927.

My mother had to apply for the Poor Relief.

I remember vividly her getting me some new trousers when I was 12 with the Provident clothing check and saying that I should have to manage with those that year. Hopefully she would get me the jacket next year.

She also used to get two one-penny 'tea tickets' from a local shop (Althams) each week when she shopped. She saved these up and exchanged them for a half-day excursion ticket to Cleethorpes.

Our one weekly treat, on 'Relief' day, Thursday, was a night at the local Kinema. The tram fares were 3d, cinema 7d, mint rock 2d, bar of Bournville chocolate 2d. The total cost 1/2d (6p in today's money!).

One of her favourite sayings used to be: "What can't be cured must be endured". She certainly lived up to that.

She loved walking, night or day time, flowers, trees, lovely gardens, parks, hymns and music hall songs.

It's 51 years since she died. I still miss her terribly and constantly wish that I could have done much more to help her and ease her burden while she was alive. But that is fate. I salute her memory and will always be grateful for all she did for me.

Eric Carey, Sheffield

'She bought me drawing books with pictures to copy'

I THOUGHT my mum was great. She had a little desk and as I loved pencils and paper she taught me the letters of the alphabet and then I graduated to two and three-letter words. She also bought me drawing books with pictures to copy.

She and father used to take me on Saturday evenings to the town centre in Huddersfield. The shops used to sell off their fruit cheap on Saturday nights and so we had plenty for

Sunday and the rest of the week.

On Sunday evenings in the summer the whole family went for a walk through the fields. In the winter months we would have a sing-song round the piano with my mother playing.

They were very happy days and I loved my parents dearly.

Ella Pearson, Chatham

'It's better than a smack in the face with a wet lettuce'

My mother was born in 1892 and lived through two world wars. She was the kindest, gentlest and most helpful person I have ever known. Not just to me and my sisters but to everyone she met.

She taught me many things with her wise sayings, such as "The best way to teach is by example," and, "If you cannot say anything good of a person say nothing at all," and, "Don't measure other people by your own yardstick".

She also had funny sayings, like "Well, it's better than a smack in the face with a wet lettuce," if something turned up that wasn't worth much.

She was poor and uneducated but she had a wealth of wisdom and much more common sense than many of today's intellectuals.

Her accomplishments were many. She could sew, knit, cook, ride a bike, supply meals for us all for a week on something like 1s 6d, but above all she could laugh and sing. She had much sorrow and tragedy in her life, but with her bright blue eyes she smiled through it all.

Wherever we lived, and we lived in many places, neighbours soon discovered that if anyone was sick or in trouble they only had

31

to call on my mum and it would all be taken care of.

She taught me tolerance and never to judge other people, and to have compassion for others, but importantly, for myself too. Through her I know the value of humility and of the ability to laugh at myself.

Although she died in 1980 I still feel mum is with me, and I shall love her until the day I die.

Jean Walker, Chester

'A legend in her lifetime'

WHO WORE blue corduroy slacks with her hair tied up in a turban ready to cycle miles to get us 'treats' during rationing? Who made us siren suits out of remnants so that we could be snug and warm when sitting under the stairs (next to the pickled eggs) during the air raids? Why mum, of course.

Bessie Ann, who looked more like our big sister than our mother, whose death devastated us and who left a legacy of common sense, fun, energy and stamina that will remain with us always.

A born optimist, mother never considered anything impossible and took to running the village shop, with no previous experience, at almost 40 and learning to drive in her 50s. In fact she never stopped learning, tackling new skills with patience and cheerfulness.

A constant source of encouragement to my sister and I in whatever we did, with an insistence that whatever we started we must finish, gave us confidence and an early independence.

An ability to make snap decisions (with no post mortems) and her workaholic nature, made her a surprised successful business woman in her late middle age. We all benefited from her unobtrusive generosity.

A legend in her lifetime, Bessie is still remembered by many people in the Midlands village where she lived, but to my sister and I and our children she was a truly wonderful mother and grandmother.

Marlene Neep, Woking

Opposite: Bessie Ann aged 11 in 1924,
dressed as Jackie Coogan in the village hospital parade

'The children loved her steamed ginger puddings'

HER NAME was Ava Maria and she left school at 11 to work in domestic service. Her schooldays were spent learning to knit and sew and for written work she had to take her own slate and three old pennies.

Eventually she married and had eight children. To help with the housekeeping she used to go out to work locally. She would help to deliver babies and if there was a bereavement she would do the laying out.

She was one of the first people to cook school dinners. These had to be prepared at home and then she had a trolley to wheel them down to the village school. There she had to serve them and afterwards do all the washing up.

The children loved her steamed ginger puddings and always came back for more.

She always used to say "neither borrow or lend", which proved good advice throughout my married life.

Marian Burton, Goole

'We were all thrilled to have an inside toilet'

SHE HAD beautiful red hair, which I always envied, and lovely amber eyes. She was beautiful both in looks and nature. She had a fiery temper, but when she smacked us we had always deserved it.

In the First World War she was working six looms at the cotton mills in Manchester. All four of her brothers fought in the war and one was killed.

We were born in a little terraced house in Manchester, but in 1938 moved to a modern flat. We were all thrilled to have a real bathroom and inside toilet.

When the Second World War started dad was called up and the children were evacuated. She was so sad to leave them. There was only mum and I in the flat, we were very close to each other then.

I would often put my arms round her and tell her I loved her. I'm so glad now that I did as sadly she died at the early age of 54.

Jean Young, Blackpool

TERRY THOMAS said that his mother tried to speak like a well-behaved duchess. When he was a boy he hated having to introduce some of his relations to his friends, "Apart for my mother and sister, I was ashamed of the lot of them". He also mentioned their drinking habits. "My father liked getting sloshed. While he was exclusively a whisky-and-soda man, my mother did not specialise. She drank anything. Regularly. But I never once saw her anywhere near intoxicated. Well-behaved duchesses naturally took great care never to be seen tiddly."

MY CHILDREN ARE MY LIFE

'There must have been times when she almost reached screaming point, but I never once heard her complain'

M Y MOTHER was always there for me. And even through the hard times I could always count on her. In fact we all could. There were six of us, four girls and two boys.
I was the eldest. Her first born to her second husband in 1935.

She was 36 when she gave birth to me, and within the next ten years she had five more children two of whom were twins. Hers was a hard life. But she always appeared to be happy and content with her lot.

It wasn't until I was older that I began to notice that all was not as it appeared to be. I learned of the many winters she had walked to the shops in deep snow, with cardboard in her shoes to cover the holes which let in the cold and the wet.

I also learned how she had gone without food in order to feed us, and of the days when she was lucky and she actually ate porridge three times in one day. It was then I knew that over the years she had really been crying on the inside. From that day on, I tried to help wherever I could.

My mother never thought of herself. She thought only of her children and where the next meal was coming from. Whenever friends asked her why she never went out and enjoyed herself, she would answer, "My children are my life. Why would I want to go out and leave them?".

There must have been times when she almost reached screaming point, but I never once heard her complain.

We lived in a house with only one large room on the ground floor. And in that room, mother did everything. For instance, she cooked for eight of us on the old one-ringed cooker which stood in the corner of the room, and alternated the two heavy cast-iron pans between that and the rib of the coal fire.

Bread, cakes and pastry - when she could afford the ingredients - were baked on the square, white-topped table with the leg-of-mutton legs which stood in the centre of the room, and she baked in the fire oven of the old black-leaded range.

On those days, you could smell the baking half way down the street and it certainly made my mouth water.

Monday was always washing day. We took it in turns to grab the clothes as they came out of the mangle, all dolly-blued and crispy white. When the basket was full, mother took them outside and hung them across the street on the clothes line to dry.

For us, those were happy days. We knew nothing of life and its miseries.

In those days, every street had its rows and rows of squeaky-clean washing flying about in the breeze, and the smell of clean fresh air, when it was brought indoors, is a smell I have never forgotten.

But I also remember the day the coal-man came, and accidentally touched mother's clean white sheet with his sack as he passed. I had never seen her so cross and she told him off and sent him away with a flea in his ear.

After tea on Monday evening, she tackled the tall pile of ironing. This, also, she did on the white-topped table.

By the time she was finished, there was just enough time for a mug of steaming-hot cocoa before going to bed.

There was always work to do. If she wasn't darning socks, she was cutting and turning sheets. And when she wasn't doing that she was sewing clothes for one of us. She never sat still for very long.

Friday night was bath-night when the long tin bath was taken down from its hook on the wall and placed in front of the fire, where we all had our weekly bath. Once again, the water was ladled out of the boiler with a ladling-can and the bath was filled. Afterwards, father dragged it to the door to empty it outside into the gutter.

On Saturday mornings, my sisters and I had to scrub the attic stairs and the attic bedrooms from top to bottom and then we did the outside steps and donkey-stoned them all.

We weren't allowed to be idle. By the time I was fourteen, I was pushing the cart to the coal-yard and bringing back a sack of coal 'eggs' for the fire.

But when the slump came there were no more coal 'eggs' on a Saturday morning. We had to make do with logs from the woods whenever we could get them. And as there was very little money about, mother made soup from potatoes and onions for dinner, followed by dripping and bread for tea.

Sometimes, if we could afford extra milk, we had rice-pudding with nutmeg. I remember one such day when we all sat down to eat and thoroughly enjoyed our meal, all except mother that is, who said she had already eaten. It was much later when I found out that in fact she hadn't eaten at all that day, because there wasn't enough to go round.

Yes, times were hard, but mother always managed to make something out of nothing for her six children. She would even invite our friends in, when we were lucky enough to have stew and dumplings. "There's plenty. Come in and sit down, love. Don't be shy," she would say. Then she would sit beside the fire with a bowl of porridge made from oatmeal.

Mother could never turn anyone away. She was so kind. Even though we didn't have much, she was always willing to share the little we had with others.

But there were happy times too. During the winter months when the days were short, we would sit beside the fire while mother, sitting on her high-backed chair, taught us to sing the hymns she had learned as a child, while father dozed in his armchair. She loved to sing, even though she didn't have much to sing about.

She taught us all to knit and to do corkwork. We sat for hours, lifting the wool over the tacks in the bobbin. It was a game to us, and we would have a contest to see who could make the longest chain, when there was cheering for the winner, who received two-ounces of dolly mixtures from mother.

Come the Christmas season, we all made paper-chains and stuck them together with flour-paste. We then painted them with our sixpenny box of paints and strung them across the ceiling.

But Christmas Eve was the night we looked forward to most of all - when mother hung six stockings on the bedpost and filled them with an apple, an orange and a bag of peanuts.

I remember one very special Christmas when mother made all the girls a doll from dolly-pegs and she knitted an outfit for each one and used pipe cleaners for the arms, and father carved an engine for each of the boys from an old piece of wood and painted them green and red.

We were so excited that day and played with our new toys for hours. As poor as we were, we never missed out on anything if mother could help it.

Even on Pancake Tuesday, we watched as mother tossed pancakes for tea and we ate them with warm syrup. Easter time, we had four Easter sun-bonnets, and the boys had a sun-hat each, all made by her own fair hand.

And somehow we all had shiny new shoes to show off at Whitsuntide. We never knew how she managed it, but she did.

Then there were the times when one of us was ill, and she made up one of her herbal concoctions. Most of the time they worked too. Goodness knows what would have happened had they not worked, because we couldn't afford doctors' bills. So we were very lucky that herbal medication came easy to mother. She knew so much about herbs and their uses.

Summer saw the start of her sarsparilla blood tonic. "It will help to cool your blood," she would say. And her lemon drink would help to slake our thirst, she would tell us, smiling. And it did too. We trusted her judgement implicitly in such matters, and we were never ill for very long.

On bath-night our hair was washed with rosemary which she found in the hedgerows. And to the rinsing water was added a dash of vinegar. People often commented on the condition of our hair. She was so proud of her brood.

She never went to bed before eleven o'clock, but was always up with the lark next day, rain or shine. She'd be out collecting herbs or scrubbing the flags, or some such task. I really don't know where she found the energy. My mother didn't have a grammar-school education, but she was full of knowledge, and it's all thanks to her that we are what we are today.

To me she will always be a saint and I loved her more than words can say. I only wish that she was here today to read this. It would really make her feel that all her efforts were not in vain.

Frances Newall-Smith, Bingley

MAKING ENDS MEET

'Mother said she could not have so many animals in one room'

FOR AN income mother let some of the rooms in our eight-roomed rented house. We often had artists from Collins Music Hall, a few yards from us.

We had a few odd lodgers. One man came with a dozen performing dogs, but mother said she could not have so many animals in one room.

Another man had a number of midgets, but there was such a crowd of sightseers outside our front door - as midgets were rather an unusual sight - mother said later that we did not want that again.

We had many laughs as I got older. When we started laughing the dog would join in.

The dog was allowed to sleep outside my room as it was in the attics. Mother, in the basement, seemed a long way away.

Mother taught us to work hard, be honest, never be libellous about anyone, say thank you for everything we were given, and say our prayers each night.

Ivy Banwell, Harrow

'She was a Trojan and worked to keep us all together'

THERE were eight of us to bring up when my father died in 1932. People came to see my mother from the welfare and wanted her to put the three youngest children in an orphanage, but she absolutely refused.

As my father had worked on the men's conveniences, my mother was offered a job on the ladies' conveniences, as at that time they only employed widows.

40

*Sarah, the writer's mother, aged 42, and (standing from left to right)
Jean (10), Agnes (11), Lilly (9), Elsie (3³/₄). Frank (2³/₄) is sitting on
his mother's lap alongside Andrew (6)*

She worked two shifts, 7am to 3pm and 3pm to midnight, six days a week on and six days a week off. For this she was paid 30/- a week.

In spite of the shortage of cash my mother insisted that as the children reached 14 and left school they went on to continuation school at the Lister Institute. She insisted that a good education was as important for the girls as it was for the boys.

She was always smiling and singing and many of the songs I sang to my own children were learned from her.

It wasn't as though she was used to hardship; her own family had been tradespeople and she had been well educated. But she was a Trojan and worked to keep us all together.

Elsie Succamore, Wickford

'In spite of all these hard times, my dear mum kept her lovely sense of humour'

DAD WAS a miner and at 32 he had an accident and his spine was fractured. This marked the beginning of tough times for my brave mother with two children to rear and a husband unable to work.

There was no room for false pride in her life - only justified pride in keeping our family ship afloat and never ever getting into debt.

She worked for other people every day cleaning and dressmaking, and every evening I remember her working to keep our house spick and span.

We had pegged rugs on the floor which we all helped to make. I remember cutting up the pieces of material ready for use and we had big discussions about the patterns we would have using the prettier colours.

In spite of all these hard times my dear mum kept her lovely sense of humour and lived to be 92. She married for the second time when she was 78 and enjoyed her later years to the full.

I thank God for her example.

Doris Reeve, Eastwood

'She tells us of going to work at six in the morning to clean a pub'

MY MUM has been totally deaf since she was 14. She brought us three children up to be honest and hard working.

My mum worked hard all her life doing part-time jobs. She often tells us of going to work at six in the morning to clean a pub and leaving us in bed as my dad was on nights and hadn't come home yet.

Mum always managed to save some money so we could go on days out or on holidays - only cheap caravan holidays, but what fun!

She is 79 now and though she has arthritis she still does what she can about the house.

We all love her very much.

Diane Townsend, Coventry

'Mrs Jenkins came to the rescue with her daughter's ballerina dress'

I WAS THE youngest girl with four brothers and four sisters. My father was unable to work for two years due to a spinal disorder, so my mother helped with the cleaning at a nearby dairy.

Her employer, Mrs Jenkins, very kindly gave mother toys and clothes which her daughter had outgrown. These came in handy as I was two years younger.

I was the 'lucky child' chosen by the school to attend the Kensington Lord Mayor's Fancy Dress Ball. My mother couldn't afford a fancy dress but Mrs Jenkins came to the rescue with her daughter's ballerina dress.

I felt very special travelling on the No 52 bus with my mother, all wrapped up in a blanket.

When father was working, he didn't get paid until Saturday evening. Mother would go shopping to Portobello Road. Meat would be sold off cheaply and she would struggle home, with the help of my older sister, laden with goodies. We would wait patiently for a treat.

While she was shopping father would bath us in the tin bath in front on the kitchen fire.

My mother was trained as a court dressmaker so we were very fortunate that she was able to make our clothes including coats with matching hats designed by father.

Holidays were out of the question - a bus trip to Kensington Gardens and the Serpentine was something special. Mother would take us jam sandwiches and fizzy lemonade.

Margaret Coles, Dawlish

Margaret's parents, husband and sons Christopher and Andrew

Ethel's sister, mother and herself, in nurses' uniform

'I can still remember the soft fluffy whiteness of the toy rabbits'

D AD, being a writer, was not very consistent regarding finance so mother did her best to keep the family going. At a time when it was unthinkable for women to work outside the home in anything other than domestic posts, my mum became a rep for various companies. Having no car, she made her way by bicycle.

Before this venture she put her skills to anything to earn much-needed cash.

Her needlework skills were phenomenal! I can still remember the soft fluffy whiteness of the toy rabbits she made. They were soon snapped up by enthusiastic customers. The jolly golliwogs dressed in bright jackets and trousers were another of her creations, plus the beautifully-dressed rag dolls.

Her cookery expertise resulted in the sale of mounds of cream horns bulging with jam and melt-in-the-mouth pastry, squares of delicious toffee, boxes of coconut ice, fudge and Turkish delight.

Her accomplishments were never-ending - from being the family hairdresser, to doing any necessary painting and decorating.

Her faith in our ability to do anything we wanted was a beacon which guided us through the turmoils of growing up. We couldn't let her down.

One particularly poignant memory is of the way mother tried to brighten up my sister and I on our first Christmas away from home.

We were training as nurses in a TB sanatorium in Ashford, Kent and had just come off the night shift, feeling dispirited and homesick.

We were greeted by this indomitable woman who had cycled all the way from Whitstable over the snow-covered ground to bring us a glimpse of home with a huge iced cake, which we were able to share with our fellow nurses, and a bag of presents.

Ethel Rayment, Bexleyheath

'A 1920s version of an Angry Young Man swept her off her feet'

MOTHER was a short, plump, very religious, quiet lady with a gentle smile, who was swept off her feet by a 1920s version of an Angry Young Man. Eccentric and artistic, he couldn't keep her, or we three children, in a suitable manner so she had to go out to work.

This was something no other mother I knew had to do. Married women then just did not go out to work.

In retrospect her day was sheer slavery. She had to travel seven miles to her position as a cashier in a drapery shop, leaving home at

7am to go by bus and train, and didn't get back until seven at night.

God knows how she coped with all the cooking, housework, washing and mending. She must have suffered agonies wondering whether we'd got off to school all right and whether we'd got our dinner, for there were no school meals then. We had to walk home and back again.

How did she find time to get me, an avid reader, into the local library at an unusually early age, instil in us all the Ten Commandments, or attend to my eldest brother's entry into the local grammar school?

Helen J Zielonko, Derby

'She had a name for being one of the best pickers'

ORN IN 1888, mother lived to be 92 and worked hard all her married life. At the outbreak of the war in 1914 (when I was only two), my father opted to register as a conscientious objecter and offered to work on food growing.

He was directed to a large market garden in Sussex. A small cottage was available - water came from an outside tap, we had oil lamps and an earth closet.

My mother kept the place spotless and was always available to help if needed in other people's houses for occasional jobs.

But most of all she liked the fruit picking season. She had a name for being one of the best pickers. The fruit went for jam for the Forces.

At the end of the war my father was offered a large, army dining-hall-type hut on an island at Chertsey on the Thames.

They turned it into a tea room and food shop. Boats on the river would stop for tea and those living on houseboats were glad to get supplies there.

One of my tasks was to turn the handle of the ice-cream machine.

Eventually they took over a vegetarian guest house. It had a large garden and eight or nine bedrooms. Mother did all the cooking, made her own bread, did most of the housework, including taking hot water up to each bedroom (and emptying the slops!).

They were well-known and popular with visitors. When the owner finally sold the property they retired gracefully to a small flat after a long, hard life.

My mother's principles were well instilled into me: keep oneself clean and tidy, speak properly and never be rude or noisy.

What a wonderful mother I had.

Joan Scott, Colwyn Bay

ROBERT MORLEY

said that after her marriage his mother had to learn how to manage - to learn for the first time that dishes had to be cleaned after a meal, fires lighted after they've gone out, that beds required making and potatoes peeling. She also dreaded the feeling of insecurity in her marriage.

How she ever came to marry Robert's father, and why, were questions he longed to ask her.

His parents separated when he was 16. In some ways this made things easier for his mother, but he felt that she probably regretted the decision.

She never spoke about it, but she did constantly refer to the loss, at about the same time, of a canteen of cutlery which Robert's father, after one of his financial crises, had either sold or pawned.

In later life she became obsessed with this feeling of deprivation and would say, "If only, dear, we still had the canteen".

Robert felt it would have been useless to point out to her that even if she still had it, it would probably have been in store. For her the canteen had become a symbol of the security which women of her generation had come to expect.

PROUD TO PLAY HER PART

'I was not allowed to read anything except what my mother referred to as Sunday books'

ALTHOUGH I was born in the 1920s, I was brought up in a very Victorian manner. Perhaps the reason was that my mother was in her Forties when I was born and my grandmother before that was in her forties when my mother was born.

Mother was a very smartly dressed, good-looking woman - piano teacher, organist at our village church and, before I was born, teacher at the school.

Naturally I had to learn to play the piano and was taught my reading, writing and arithmetic by mother, not starting school until I was six.

On Sundays I was not allowed to play any games or sew, knit or read anything except what my mother referred to as 'Sunday' books.

Mother organised our church concerts and so the various turns were practised in our house in the evenings with mother playing the piano accompaniments.

When our church harvest festival auction sale took place, mother acted as auctioneer's clerk. The money was donated to the Leicester Royal Infirmary.

Mother was such a busy woman for, apart from running our large house, she attended to the flower gardens, looked after the poultry and helped with father's book-keeping when he was the village builder, joiner and undertaker.

Also, as father was clerk to the parish council, she attended to the sending out of the allotment bills to the allotment holders.

Father liked 'a drink', but mother, who never touched a drop except for a very small toast at weddings, would lose her temper

with father if he had been to one - or both - of our village pubs, or had had a drink of potent homemade wine at the home of a friend or customer.

Oh, the rows which ensued then between my parents! Thank goodness it didn't happen often.

When the four daughters of the millionaire who lived at the local hall were, each in turn, married, mother was invited to play the organ at the village church for the services.

As these were important 'society' weddings mother was very proud and delighted to have been chosen instead of the Leicester Cathedral organist.

When I was a small child mother brought me up to always refer to people as 'a lady' or 'a gentleman'. I taught my two daughters to do the same.

Another thing I was told by her was that it was bad manners to pass remarks in peoples' houses about any articles I saw there.

Mother was, alas, killed in a car accident.

Through the long years which have followed, in spite of my having a very happy marriage and two lovely daughters, I have missed having a loving mother with whom I could share my joys and sorrows.

Laura Fost, Ammanford, Dyfed

JOYCE GRENFELL'S
mother wrote to her from America saying she wished her daughter would occasionally look a little less unglamorous in the parts she played in films.

Picture after picture reached her local 'movie-house' with Joyce playing gawky girls failing to get their man. Joyce's mother did wish that her friends could see her in a more becoming guise!

When she was coming to Britain to visit her daughter she told a new acquaintance at her table on board ship that Joyce would be in the film they were going to see that evening.

As usual Joyce looked plain and awkward and her mother's heart sank.

When the lights went up at the end of the picture her companion asked which was her daughter.

Her mother said she'd made a mistake and her daughter wasn't in that particular film after all.

In The Million Pound Note, with Gregory Peck, Joyce played an Edwardian duchess in beautiful clothes. Her mother told all her friends to go and see that.

A HOME FULL OF LOVE

'My father helped her to give the love and happiness she had never enjoyed herself'

MY MOTHER was everything I could have wished for had I been able to choose my own parents. Having lost her own mother in childbirth and her father at sea, she had an extremely hard and loveless life until she met and married my good father.

He helped her to give to her three children the love and happiness she had never enjoyed herself.

She literally shared our lives, played with us, skipped and ran with us, sang with us. She was always there, our sympathetic confidente, our adviser, our encourager.

Through her example we learned to know right from wrong, patience and perseverence.

My great regret is that she had no mother to turn to for help, as we turned instinctively to her.

When my husband says: "You're just like your mother" that is a compliment second to none.

He should know; motherless himself, she became a very special mother-in-law to him.

Mary Padget, Hatfield

'We had our Christmas dinner one week late'

MY MOTHER was just another working man's wife and mother of us three children in the years between the two wars.

Dad was often unemployed but everything at home remained as always - there was warmth and love.

One particular Christmas, when I suppose things were blacker than usual, we were told, "Father Christmas won't be coming this year". I remember the feeling I had when I woke up on Christmas morning and found out that there were no presents for us, particularly as Christmas Eve is my birthday!

We had meat pudding for dinner but the following week, at new year, mum went to the market and was able to afford a turkey - butchers didn't have refridgeration in those days - so we had our Chrismas dinner one week late.

The photograph shows her when she was a delegate at a conference when she was 84. The dog is not hers, just a friendly pooch who came up to her and she spoke to it.

Mrs Gee, Romford

'Her pastry was quite delicious, as light as a feather'

M Y GRANDMOTHER was the best mum I could have had. I was born in October 1918 and my mother died the same day so my dear gran, who I always called mum, cared for me together with my kindly grandfather.

My gran's was an open house to her many friends. She took a delight in making homemade jam and wine and we would gather blackberries and elderberries from the forest.

Her cooking was superb, her pastry quite delicious, as light as a feather, and friends often dropped in for tea.

She was always there when I came home from school. Homeward bound on a wet, wintry day I recall opening the door to a cosy house with the smell of some delicious meal filling the kitchen and warming the cockles of my heart.

The joy of entering a house which this good woman had turned into a home has remained with me throughout the years.

Mum was a true Christian. She would give a helping hand to anyone at any time and I never heard her say a bad word about anybody.

She endured hardships for most of her life, but she was never bitter. Full of kindness and compassion and generosity, she had a wonderful sense of humour.

Life's many challenges and hardships served to make her stronger and more resourceful.

Rosemary Young, Ashford

HAPPINESS AND WISE WORDS

'If I were naughty
she had only to look at me'

SHE WAS a sweet and loveable person who, as I grew older, was a friend as well as a mother. She never smacked me - she used to say if I were naughty she had only to look at me, and I stopped!

I was always taught to stand up in a bus or tram if anyone elderly hadn't a seat.

Mother used to make nearly all my clothes. I can remember red and green velvet dresses with swansdown trimming round the neck and sleeves. If anything got too short she would put a contrasting piece on the edge of the hem.

She made her own hats. There was a very pretty one of navy chiffon ruched at the top and a black lace-trimmed one with a lovely

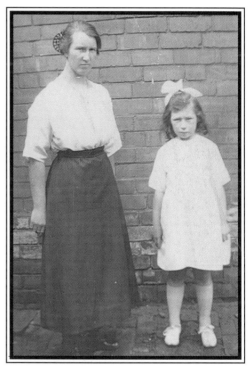

Mother and myself when I was about eight. Don't I look sulky! But I didn't like having my photo taken

pink rose at the side.

She was a good cook and I remember her saying, "If you're hard up, or left on your own, see that you get one good meal a day - you can manage on bread and jam for other meals".

When I was a teenager and stopped going to church she said, "I'm not going to press you to go, I am saying don't stop saying your prayers each day. If you are worried about anything, tell God about it and He will help you through".

I'm sure it was that faith that helped dear Mum through many a hard time and it has helped me too.

Twenty years ago I wrote her this poem for Mother's Day...

Mother dear, whose life to me
A constant joy has been,
I give you thanks for all the years
Of happiness I've seen.

For all the care you took of me
Throughout my childhood days,
For all the sweet, wise words you spoke,
And all your loving ways.

And as I think of you this day
I pray the long years through
May bring God's blessings in their train
Mother dear, to you.

Norah Griffiths, Doncaster

DREAMS WERE ALL I HAD

'She told us about how lovely everything was going to be next year'

MY MOTHER gave birth to 12 children and raised 11 - seven boys and four girls. Our father, despite all those children, was an 'absent husband'. He spent more time away from home than in it.

Looking back, I realise how lonely and unhappy my mother was with no-one to confide in or to offer her comfort and support. Money was very short and at times she was at her wits end, not knowing how we would survive from one day to the next.

She was always positive with us children - always thinking up different ways to keep us entertained and cheerful - especially when she had no supper to give to us.

She would sit us in a semi-circle around the fire and lead us in singing. As the smaller children fell asleep, she carried them off to bed.

When just we older children were still awake she sat and talked to us. She told us about how lovely everything was going to be next year - the picnics we would have.

Oh, how we planned those picnics. The food was the most important of course and we argued over the merits of jam tarts as opposed to cheesecakes. Sometimes mother would relax the rules and say that it might not be too greedy to have both. How we shivered with delighted sinfulness. Lots of dreams my mother had, but 'next year' never came.

When I was a grown woman and a mother myself, I asked her, "How could you go on with your dreams, year after year?".

She answered, "Dreams were all I had, my dear. They were what kept me going, the hope for the future".

The special thing about my mother was her courage.

Josephine McCallow, Brentwood

SECURITY AND UNDERSTANDING

'If tears were shed she was there to comfort and love us'

SHE WAS gentle, sweet and a lady. She never raised her voice, and so we were gentle with others, too. If tears were shed she was there to comfort and love us. She helped each one of us in our different ways and tried to give us what we needed, though times were hard.

To be alive was a pleasure for her.

Eileen Kirby, Tunbridge Wells

'I watched fascinated as they made themselves into twigs'

MY MOTHER loved nature and wanted us to share this love. I remember her showing me some stick insects she had noticed on a bush. I watched fascinated as they made themselves into 'twigs'. On another walk she showed us a 'robin's pincushion' on some wild roses.

Although a busy person - I was a child in the 1920s - she used to take us on walks and picnics and read us a chapter of a story book before we went to bed.

She gave us security and a happy childhood. I have so many happy memories. I've tried to recreate that atmosphere for my children, and they in turn, for theirs.

Annette Haynes, Malmesbury

'She would dress our dolls and tell us wonderful stories'

AT THE age of 22 my mother was a widow with two children. I wasn't born until two months after my father's ship was blown up.

Though it was a great struggle through the years that followed on her meagre naval pension, we had all the love and care that she could give us.

She made us pretty dresses and earnt a few shillings making them for others. With the little pieces left over she would dress our dolls and tell us wonderful stories while we sat watching her.

She was so patient and full of fun. When I was seven she married the dearest man who cared for us as though we were his own.

The grandchildren thought her great fun and there was giggling for hours when she stayed with us.

When she died in her sleep aged 92 she left a big empty gap in many of our lives.

Peggy Ballard, Towcester

'Beautiful dinners would appear from a few bacon bones'

MEMORIES of my lovely mother are so very precious to me. I never once heard her complain about hardship. The love in the house when mum was there was indescribable, she always seemed to make everything right.

How she fed and clothed us I will never know - but beautiful dinners would appear from a few bacon bones and pearl barley.

I now wear her wedding ring and when I look down at it, I remember all the hard times she must have known. I can only hope that in her twilight years I was able to give her just a half of all the love and happiness she gave to me.

Eileen Cooper, Brentwood

AN EXAMPLE TO EVERYONE

'Over the years
I have tried to pattern myself on her'

REMEMBERING my mother always gives me a warm feeling. When I was a young girl back in the 1920s she made me feel that I was special.

My brothers and I loved our father dearly but between mother and us there was something different, we were so much closer to her somehow.

She was a true Yorkshire woman: hardworking, honest and with a warm, loving nature. Over the years I have tried to pattern myself on her. I hope that what she taught me has rubbed off onto my children.

I am 73 now with 15 children, around 60 grandchildren and great grandchildren. If only she could have lived to see them all.

Mrs Edith Abbey, Norton-on-Derwent

'The lodgers skipped
off without
paying the rent'

I WAS just 10 months old when my father, who'd been blind for a year, died leaving my mother with six children. Unknown to my mother, my father's sister, trying to be helpful, arranged for all the children (except me, the baby) to be adopted. My father's sister was furious when my mother refused to let the children go and said she was selfish and would end up in the workhouse. She replied, "Then we'll all go there together".

My mother managed to keep the family house going for a short while by taking in lodgers, but more often than not they skipped off without paying the rent. We eventually moved to a small flat.

She cooked everything on the old black kitchen range. How well I remember the red glow of the fire. And what warmth and comfort it brought to us all, especially when we'd been poorly.

I never saw my mother sitting down without knitting or sewing in her hands. All our underclothes were hand-knitted. I still remember the hills and valleys on my sit-upon from knitted combs and knickers.

My own five children have all turned out well, due I'm sure to the values she instilled in me and which I in turn have passed on to them: hard work, perseverance, cheerfulness, having a go, never getting into into debt, never envying anybody and being thankful for what the Good Lord has given you.

Laura Howell, St Albans

'She kept us supplied with jam sandwich doorsteps'

S HE WAS a lovely lady - honest, kind, unselfish and always ready to do anyone a good turn. She was also great fun - prepared at a minute's notice to leave her household chores and make us cakes, coconut ice and toffee apples.

She would take my brother and me, together with our friends to visits places of interest, museums and the zoo.

She welcomed our friends and kept us supplied with jam sandwich doorsteps, home-made lemonade or jugs of tea.

At the same time she would stand no nonsense and we knew when she said anything she meant it!

I thank God for her and only wish I'd shown her how much I loved her while she was alive.

Rebecca Jennings, London SE18

'Always there to help us, to cheer us up when we were down'

MY PARENTS were Polish immigrants who fled from the pogroms on the Jews at the turn of the century. They arrived in London with three small children, my mother pregnant with the fourth. She had married at sixteen, so she was still in her twenties. They had very little money, no home and not a word of English between them.

In the years that followed our family grew to eleven children, my brother and I being twins.

As hard as her life inevitably was, I never remember my mother being other than cheerful and optimistic, always there to help us, to cheer us up when we were down.

We were all treated by her as individuals and she encouraged us to follow our own paths - which was rare in those days - to be self-reliant and to work hard.

Her great ambition was for all her brood to benefit from a good education and become worthwhile British citizens.

Alhough without education herself, she was intelligent and very forward-thinking, learning politics from the wireless and later the television.

At one period she even fed us all on natural foods only, after hearing a lecture on it which fired her imagination many years before such ideas were popular.

This is part of an essay my granddaughter Caron wrote when she was eleven (the subject was The Person You Most Admire): 'Booba (as we all call her) was called the Queen Bee and her home was the hive. Her children, grandchildren and great grandchildren were the bees who swarmed around it'.

Gertrude Denenberg, Westcliffe-on-Sea

SHIRLEY TEMPLE BLACK

remembers her mother as a homemaker who made all their clothes. Her parents didn't really have any ambition for their daughter, it just happened.

Shirley's mother was mostly German with a little English blood, so life at home was disciplined, "a lot of fun, but we had a lot of rules and regulations".

When people admired her daughter, Shirley's mother used to say, "Isn't it nice that she can make people happy?" and left it at that. For that her daughter is very grateful.

When she first started appearing in films, the young Shirley couldn't read so her mother would sit by her bed at night and would read the scenes for the following day.

Shirley would listen to them, maybe repeating them a couple of times before going to sleep. By the morning she'd know them.

SEEING MUM IN A DIFFERENT LIGHT

'She was prettier than all the flowers I have ever seen'

ONE WET day my sister and I were plaguing our father, a London taxi driver, to tell us how he met mum, and this is what he said (by the way, he was a man who rarely said anything 'soft' or even nice!):

"One day when we were young, me and me mates took a bike ride down to Kent. We sat down outside a farm to eat our grub and I looked through the hedge and saw a girl who was sweeping the yard. She was just like a morning flower, with the dew still on her, and I just could not take my eyes away.

"I tried to call out (as was the London way) but she just blushed and turned away, hurrying indoors.

"After that I used to go down there every weekend, but alone of course, and, by doing little jobs for him, got to know the farmer who was her father. A long time later I said I wanted to marry her."

After much consideration - they were not very sure about their little girl marrying a 'foreigner' (a Londoner), and the fact that he would have to take her to that sinful city meant lots of talk - eventually all was arranged.

One day Edith and George stood in the little chapel - he with hair slicked down and an unaccustomed collar and tie on, and she in her best Sunday frock, with a bouquet of spring flowers.

What a pity that photographs were only for 'the nobs', for I should love to have been able to see it. Anyway, the marriage was a great success and she changed from the quiet-voiced country girl to a Londoner who could give as good as she got.

My dad went on, "Yer mum was prettier than all the flowers I have ever seen," and, patting her arm, "just look at her now, just as lovely and as fresh".

I looked at my mum with eyes that had never seen her before. I saw a short, dumpy woman, not really fat, but solid, with red raw hands from all the scrubbing she did, grey hair scraped back off her face into a bun, and not very tidily tied at the back.

The long black skirt which made her look about sixty, the flat shoes which had been slit to accommodate her bunions, the rolled-up sleeves and the mottled arms, thought of her short temper, and her now-raucous London voice. Just for a second I saw her as my dad did.

When I was older I realised that they must have been very much in love and I am always glad that I did, just that once, see her as she had been, and in dad's eyes, still was.

'Bunny' Parker

("I know it's a silly nickname, but I've had it now for over 75 years so I think it might stick!")

BARRY HUMPHRIES

remembers how his mother would come into his room to hear his prayers, "a litany of gibbered 'Godblesses' in which I tried to mention everyone I knew".

He says he most enjoyed prayers when his parents were going out to the pictures or to a 'card night'.

His mother would be wearing her silver fox, its sprung tortoiseshell jaw snapped shut over its own tail and its sly glass eyes staring into his. With his nose buried in 'that musky pelt' he said his prayers in his mother's perfumed embrace.

He once wrote: "The longer I protracted my prayers, the longer I could bask in Evening in Paris, Charmosan face powder and the faint vulpine odour of her wrap".

ALMOST A COCKNEY

'She was wearing open drawers - the kind of knickers worn by Queen Victoria'

WHEN my mother returned from Wales her aunt met her at the station and inspected her closely. She was forbidden to travel upstairs on the horse bus/tram which she clearly wanted to do.

Why? Because my mother was wearing 'open drawers' - the kind of knickers worn by Queen Victoria with unsewn seams in the most important place.

My father and my mother in the dress she wore to their wedding

These were designed for travelling ladies who carried an object like a small soup tureen with a lid, in which they used to relieve themselves while travelling, or at long church services, beneath their long skirts.

My dear mother was born in East London in 1897. She always said she was almost a Cockney as Bow Bells could be heard if the wind was in the right direction.

Her mother died a few days after her birth. She was then brought up by her grandmother who died when she was nine. My mother was then sent to distant relatives in south Wales to help at their farmhouse.

She attended to the chickens and cared for the baby, as well as going to school. It must have been the first time she was adequately fed as, up to then, life had been very hard for her.

Eventually she went into service but had to give up as the black woollen stockings she had to wear brought on an allergy.

In 1914 she become a telephone operator for a London hospital. This is where she met my father. They married at a registrar's office in Liverpool and she wore a beautiful pure silk navy blue dress with pin tucks and soft gathers.

She had to give up her job once she married.

When my sister and I came along, she helped grandpa in his shop and later,

My mother as a child

because my father was unemployed during the slump, she made bread for him to take out in two large suitcases to sell.

She never seemed to rest and was always looking tired.

We never had a holiday until two of us girls were working.

She was as thin as a lath as she fed my father first, children second, and there was little left for her.

After drinking, my father would be violent and beat my dear mother up.

Eventually she was asked to take charge of the switchboard at a huge office. As only our youngest sister was still at school, she took the job on trial, staying there until she retired at 65.

My father had led my mother a terrible life. When he died aged 52, after the initial shock, she discovered she could do her own things for the first time in her life. And her health became better than it had ever been.

Joyce M Dickins, Chesterfield

IAN CARMICHAEL

says his mother was very beautiful and the apple of his father's eye.

At the time of her marriage she was small and slight, weighing under seven stone. In fact she was rarely any heavier during her entire life.

She was the same age as Ian's father, both of them being 25 when they went to the altar. Her complexion, says her son, was pure peaches and cream, a quality which was inherited by all her children and grandchildren.

Throughout her life she was passionately fond of little china figurines - particularly of ladies in crinolines and poke bonnets. She also loved pictures of old English gardens - thatched roof cottages surrounded by hollyhocks, foxgloves and delphiniums - these were tastes that somehow reflected her own personality which was petite, uncomplicated, very feminine and slightly old-world. She was always vivacious and totally unsophisticated.

Whenever Ian's parents came to visit him at boarding school, he always glowed with pride. She was, to her son, without question the most beautiful mother there.

MOTHER KNOWS BEST

'She never said "do this" or "do that"'

HOW CRAFTY mothers are - mine included! She had no need to sit us down, my sister and me, with pencil and paper to pass on her experience. Instead, daily, constantly but unobtrusively, she subtly imparted her knowledge.

Take ironing.

"Let's have a competition," she would suggest, eyeing the laundry basket and father's weekly supply of large white handkerchiefs. "We'll take turns. You girls have two each and I'll do the other three. When we've all finished, we'll put them in a row and when your father comes in, he can decide who has done the best."

Father, of course, when tackled always admitted he couldn't tell the difference and they were all beautifully ironed. From there, we were manoeuvred into a shirt ironing competition.

Take cooking. If you can read the wrapper and fight your way into a package of food these days, you can cook. But more and more, as the printing on the packages grows smaller, I rely on my mother's teaching. She never said "do this" or "do that". Knowledge was innocently fed to us (if you will pardon the pun).

"Just beat this mixture for me, dear."

'What is it?"

"A cake for tea."

"Mm. Tastes good, what's in it?"

"Just butter and sugar so far."

"How much longer?" we would ask, as arms tired.

"Until it's creamy. Then you can pop these eggs in."

"Can I put icing on?"

"Lashings," she would promise.

Or: "If you've a few minutes, just wash these greens while the water is coming to the boil, then pop them in the pan."

I knew how many minutes lapsed after a hungry father came home, glanced at the paper and washed his hands, so I knew how long I had to cook those potatoes.

Clever as she was, some jobs it was impossible to disguise. Take cleaning the silver. The elder always put the polish on. The younger rubbed it off. The same with washing up. The elder washed, the younger dried the dishes. They were simply chores that had to be got through and for which we received our pocket money. No work - no pay.

Little did we realise she wove a message into everything.

I tried the same methods with my sons and daughters alike. Did I waste my time? With fast foods, spray-on and wipe-off cleaners and drip-dry clothes, so many tasks we learnt from mother are now superfluous.

Nevertheless, something must have been retained and my grandchildren are clearly well nourished and happy.

Rita Warrener, Southport

BARBARA WINDSOR'S
father said her mother was melodramatic!
Barbara's mum and dad brought out the worst in each other and sometimes her mother's fancy clothes were hurled into the garden!
Barbara's role was pig in the middle.
Her mother always found something to pick on, usually her daughter's fine hair. She was forever spitting on it to make it curl and tying it up with a big ribbon.
One day in desperation she sent Barbara off to the hairdressers for a perm. When she came to collect her, she went bananas. Barbara's head was covered in 'puppy-dog tails' and they hadn't even bothered to take off her heavy coat and gloves so she was soaked in perspiration.
"I looked a fright!" says Barbara.

HOW DID SHE DO IT?

Rosie with her mum and grandma

'Relationships are more important than money'

MUM HATES to throw anything away, particularly food. She has a long memory and recalls the days after the war when money was tighter than it is now.

I can remember helping to pile empty jam-jars and bottles into an old push chair and going with her to the shop where they would allow her a penny or two on each one. Basically we would just exchange the jars and bottles for staple foods.

Long hours she spent at her sewing machine, making blouses or baby's nightdresses. She rarely slept before midnight, but the home work made an essential contribution to our housekeeping, for it not only enabled me to go to school decently dressed but paid for a piano lesson once a week.

How my mother found the time, I don't know, but she taught me to read before I started school. I could read pieces out of the Daily Mirror at the age of four and was introduced to the public library at six years old.

Mum told me not to compete with others, only with myself; a 'personal best' could be bettered.

"There is no such word as can't," she would say firmly. "Take the 't' off and say you can. You can do anything you want to do in life providing you work and apply yourself. Always be punctual, polite and remember names when you are introduced to anyone.

"You will achieve better results if you are gentle and pleasant than if you are aggressive. Don't worry about what other folk are doing - that has nothing to do with you. Look to your own business first."

In the Fifties, education for a girl was considered, by the establishment, to be unimportant - but not according to my mother. Education, she said, was good for its own sake - no knowledge was ever wasted.

"Educate a girl and you educate a family," she would reply to critics who questioned her sanity as she machined day and night to raise enough money for my grammar school uniform and equipment.

She encouraged me when I began to write stories and illustrate a weekly magazine made for my grandmother to read. A good percentage of her hard-earned cash was spent on pencils, paper and books for me. At the time, of course, I took it all for granted, but when my sons now behave in the same way towards me, I know that eventually they will appreciate what I try to do for them.

Mum taught me to care about other people, she being the one in her own large family who always took responsibility for the welfare of the others. I learnt, at a very early age, that family and friends were important, to consider their feelings and to treat their foibles with tolerance and, where necessary, compassion.

I have tried to make my sons aware of the beauty around them as my mother certainly succeeded in doing for me.

One evening I was woken up, wrapped in a blanket and held up to the bedroom window to behold a spectacular scene. We had a wide gauge, chicken wire fence surrounding our house and snow had settled on the lower edge of each square of the wire netting and then frozen. The moon was full and it seemed as if the whole garden was covered in diamonds.

The trees were more beautiful than any Christmas fir and the whole effect was so breathtaking that I remember it still - and the love and sensitivity of my mother that prompted the awakening of a small child to share the sight with her.

One of the things that my mother never managed to instil into my brain was the management of money. Being very unmaterialistic herself she passed on the philosophy which she believed was the correct one.

I must say that I agree with her but there are many who will not. It is more important to spend time with people than to shower them with gifts. Time is more important than money; relationships are more important than money, in fact, practically everything is more important than money - providing you have enough to keep body and soul together.

She is still near enough hopeless today with her own cash, although it is only the State Pension. She is an impulse buyer which, I can assure you, is hereditary.

She taught me to meet problems head on and that there was no logic behind running away and avoiding the issue. "There's no such thing as a problem. If you can get around it then it isn't a problem in the first place and if you cannot - than it's a fact of life and you have to live with it."

Rosie Barham, Leigh-on-Sea

MAKING THINGS SPECIAL

'My mother sang while doing her housework, although there cannot have been much incentive'

MY EARLIEST memories, having been born in 1943, were of austere surroundings but a feeling of security inside the home.

Many pre-school hours were spent sitting on my Mother's knee while she persevered with my pronunciation of "th" rather than "fr".

My mother sang while doing her housework, although there cannot have been much incentive. Times were hard and money scarce.

Manners were most important to mother and in case I forgot a "please" or "thank you", I tended to start and finish a question with the word "please". Honesty and respect were drummed into me, something I still value to this day.

I was reared to think that a woman's place was in the home and if any school friend's mother went to work, even through necessity, that child was viewed with different eyes.

Shopping was done daily, round to the small parade of individual premises, and each day had its set pattern for food, mainly due to finances.

On the way home, I can remember standing still for what seemed like hours while my mother chatted to neighbours that she met. Those were the days of children being seen but not heard!

Weekend entertainment in the summer was a long walk after tea and in the winter on Sunday listening to hymns on the radio, which always seemed so melancholy.

Nearly every year we did go to the seaside for a sparse holiday which was a rarity in those times. Looking back now, I don't know how my mother coped with it all and it must have been anything but a holiday for her. Our caravan was the smallest on the site and I still ponder as to how we managed to eat and sleep in it.

Mother always made sure that birthdays were special and friends were invited to tea.

Christmas festivities were made very special just as her mother had made them happy for her. I can still recall the pillowcase filled with presents and treats, obviously obtained at some hardship to herself. I never realised until recently that she never seemed to have any presents to open for herself. She worked so hard to give us a good time.

Most of all, the underlying feeling that remains was of my mother always being at home, solid and reliable.

Mrs Joan Milbourne, Welling

FRANKIE HOWERD
used to tell this story about how his mother taught him a valuable lesson.

Frankie and the daughter of a neighbour used to put on concerts in his back garden. He charged the local kids a farthing admission fee - not inquiring too closely where the farthings came from in that poor neighbourhood. Their wardrobe was unofficially borrowed from Frankie's parents.

During the third or fourth of these Saturday matinees Frankie's mother came round and asked what was going on.

Her son explained they were giving a concert and that the children had paid a farthing.

He expected praise, instead his mother thumped him.

"A farthing," she cried, "A farthing! How dare you rob these poor children? Give them their money back immediately".

Rob! Frankie said he was affronted even at that early age for he'd assumed that if he charged a farthing and the kids paid, he just had to be worth it. But he learnt from his mother's words a basic rule for any form of entertainment: always try to make sure that you give good value for money.

75

COURAGE AND THOUGHTFULNESS

Mum,
me
and
Martin,
our
first
son,
in
1955

'Mum liked to eat a lot of cabbage'

M Y MUM always seemed to me to be tall and dignified. In later years I knew she was not so tall, but dignified she certainly was. And hardworking.

She had eight of us and six of us were girls.

My dad must have despaired of ever having a son, until the sixth child arrived. I came next and then another boy.

Mum helped dad in the shop and coped with the problems of trying to keep a large family on a very small income.

We had a hot dinner every midday when we came from school, and a light meal at night. When my sisters began to bring home their boyfriends, they also sat at the table and somehow there was always enough for everyone. That is, all except mum and dad. They never seemed to eat until we had all finished and mum liked to eat a lot of cabbage!

Mum used to make our clothes when we were small and knitted jumpers for me to wear under my gymslip for school in winter.

I was taught how to wash my personal things and to be tidy for school. Cleanliness was next to Godliness in our home and even without a bathroom, which didn't come until just a couple of years before the Second World War, we washed down each evening or morning.

We also went to the public baths on Fridays after helping to clean the house for the weekend. We had very little pocket money, but what we had was treasured and a real treat.

My dad had to pay for five weddings between 1931 and 1937, before my turn came in 1947, and that must have been really hard.

My mum was a tower of strength to dad, with her advice and her belief in him.

When the war started and my brothers and brother-in-laws went off in the Forces, mum kept us strong and by her dignified attitude and her faith, she helped all our family.

The tragic news of the death in action of my older brother, in North Africa at the age of 22, tested my father to his limit and he had a heart attack. He was frail after that blow.

I was in the ATS by then and mum kept the family strong, and somehow kept her faith. I came out of the Forces after three and a half

Freda in her ATS uniform

years, with a shadow on my lung.

Mum nursed me and packed me off to my sister's by the seaside for fresh air. There was not much of that in London, in the dockland area.

When I was ill and had to rest in bed some years later, she collected money from all round the family for us to buy a television set, and insisted that we have it because I was confined to the house for a long time.

Her courage and thoughtfulness in the face of so many adversities is a lesson I shall never forget.

I think of her so often and try to remember all the things she taught me by her own example - moral and physical cleanliness, care and love for her children, unselfishness, and a deep and quiet love for her hardworking husband.

I have tried to be a caring mother and a loving wife. My sons are adult now and are trying to make their own way in life. They are very kind, helpful and interested in what I do. One lives nearby and the other in another town. I am always there to help in any way I can.

That is what my mum taught me and I shall always try to emulate her way of life. I have not seen anything better than her values as yet.

Freda Stone, Liverpool

OSCAR WILDE quipped, "All women become like their mothers. That is their tragedy. No man does. That's his".

LOVING AND GIVING

'My brother had to carry the washing on his bicycle and collect the money'

MY MOTHER became a widow when she was 35, my brother 13 and myself six. Her widow's pension was fifteen shillings a week and five shillings for each of us. The rent was ten shillings a week.

I never remember her grumbling, or saying, "Why me?".

But I do remember her sending me to the corner shop to get half a pound of sausages. "Take your time," she said.

But me, I ran all the way there and back. When I arrived home I saw my mother sitting at our kitchen table having a good cry.

I flung my arms around her and we cried together.

She, or course, had not expected me back so soon.

She soon set about earning some money. She became caretaker at our local chapel. She used to take me with her. As the pay was quarterly we had to have something else so she took in washing.

As there were no such things as washing machines and it was reputed that the laundry spoiled the clothes, mother had plenty of work.

When the washing was ready to go back my brother had to carry it on his bicycle, and collect the money.

The next venture was to take in visitors during the summer, and we had the same people year after year.

We only had a small house, two up, two down, no bathroom - but we managed. My brother slept in our sitting room and mother and I slept on a mattress on the floor in the kitchen.

My mother was special. When it was quiet I would say, "Tell me about dad". She would tell me how they loved each other, how nothing was ever too much trouble for him.

I used to think to myself 'If I ever get married, I shall marry someone just like him'.

Mother worked very hard and started buying things for the house. She bought a secondhand piano and I was sent to music lessons.

When she found she could play simple things by ear, we had hymn singing round the piano on a Sunday afternoon.

My mother also found time for others, like the lady down the road. She lost her husband and was left with two little girls. Mother did not only say how sorry she was, but took a basket of groceries to her, "To tide you over".

Many times she would sit up all night with people who were ill, leaving my brother and I in bed, the front door locked, till she came home in the morning to get our breakfast and get us ready for school.

My mother taught me how to cook, to make a little money go a long way, to save for a rainy day, love God and my fellow men. In fact she was a real Christian lady.

Muriel Snell, Shoeburyness

A TRUE CHRISTIAN

'She was my angel mother'

NOBLE, gentle but firm and calm in all situations, beloved and lovely, she was my angel mother. Her faithful, quiet, practical Christian faith was a shining seven-day-a-week testament to all who knew her.

Beryl Monico, Pembroke

'What courage she had'

HOW remarkable she was, what courage she had. After my father died mum managed to bring us all up with a little assistance from my grandparents.

She lived a good Christian life and passed on to us sayings like: 'If you cannot speak well of anyone, don't say anything at all' and 'Always help anyone who needs it for there will always be time to do so'.

These words and her faith have helped me bring up my own children.

Frieda Cox, Swindon

'She believed the Bible taught us the way to live'

AN ONLY child, my mother was just 14 when her adored father was lost at sea in 1917. She married at 19 and had three children. My father also went to sea, as an engineer, and was often at sea for many, many weeks at a time. Their wives, of course, were left to bring up their families alone.

*Joan's
mother aged
14 with her
father just before he
was lost at sea*

I remember mother having about 17/- per week which they had
to go down to the fishing offices to collect. I am sure that mother
must have had quite a struggle, to feed and clothe us on that small
sum.

However, each week mother would put away for Christmas as
much as she could afford: 6d weekly to the butcher, 3d for the fruit
and nut club. From the butcher we might have enough for a
chicken by Christmas. A further 6d was saved, if possible for small
presents for us children.

Holidays as we know them today were unheard of, but we did
have an annual day out to Yarmouth on the train. This included a

packet of chips for our dinner.

My mother looked after us like an angel. She never knew what it was to leave us while she had an evening out, even during the few times my father was home from sea.

I never knew her to complain about her lot although she must have often been very, very tired.

One thing I shall always be thankful to her for was that, at an early age, she sent us to Sunday School. She believed the Bible taught us the way to live and guided our morals as we grew up into adults.

We lived about a mile from the town centre and once a week she would put the two youngest of us into a rather large pram and walk all the way into town to do her shopping. Then she would push us all the way home again.

When mother died six years ago, as Christians we know that one day we shall all meet again, this we firmly believe.

We planted a rose tree in our front garden in loving memory of mother. It has bloomed wonderfully each year.

Joan Brown, Lowestoft

TONY HANCOCK, in one of the classic Hancock's Half Hour programmes said, "I thought my mother was a bad cook, but at least her gravy used to move!".

RULING WITH A ROD OF IRON

'There was always a cane by mum's chair'

NINE of us children are still living in London where we were born. We had a very happy, but hard childhood and often laugh at the things that happened when we were young.

There was always a cane by mum's chair and if one of us dared to put our elbows on the table, that cane would come down like a whiplash.

We used to go to Sunday School. One of my sisters always collected the knee rests and put them together to kneel on so that she was bigger than everyone else. She got caught at it and was given a good hiding by mum.

We always had to bring our boyfriends home for tea on Sunday night. They were always made welcome, but if one of us dared to be late in, dad was told to take his belt off to us. He never hit one of us. The belt would be taken off, and as we ran up the stairs it would hit the stair behind.

Laura Murphy, Blackheath

'We didn't need to be told twice'

MY MOTHER was widowed in 1939 with four young children to bring up. She ruled with a rod of iron. We were smacked if we were naughty. We didn't need to be told twice to do something. We had impeccable table manners and rudeness was not known in our house.

Going "green" is not new. We saved everything: string, elastic bands, buttons, paper, both brown and tissue. The tissue wrapped round oranges was special; we used it in the toilet. Not for us the newspapers cut into squares!

Shirley Harrison, Bradford

'I got a clout round the ear'

I ALWAYS thought my childhood was on the uninteresting side. Since growing up I've realised it was steady, firm and loving. To start with I didn't have a mother all that long; she died at 49 when I was 13.

The good definitely die young.

At her funeral there were 100 wreaths from friends all over. She would give her last penny to anyone worse off than herself.

Her washing was admired for miles around. But then she had good training as she was in service with Lord Mountbatten's mother, or was it grandmother?

I take after my mum as I am over-fussy and fidgety.

I remember the time I had some kids in our shed playing doctors and nurses and showing bums and willies.

I got a clout round the ear and the kids were sent home sharpish!

My sister and I later decided that we were much more understanding to our children than she was to us.

Edna Ward, Richmond

BRENDAN BEHAN is quoted as saying:
"Never throw stones at your mother,
You'll be sorry for it when she's dead,
Never throw stones at your mother,
Throw bricks at your father instead."

No Such Word as Can't

'She taught me the value
of perseverance
and the grace of patience'

IN 1933 when I was eight it took nearly a year for me to recover from an adenoid operation. It was a time of great boredom for there was no television and no video games in those days.

I used to stand at the window, looking out for my friends coming home from school.

"You need a hobby," my mother said one day. "You need to learn to do something useful."

Next morning she brought me a brown paper packet. Out fell a cascade of bright skeins of cotton - red, blue green and yellow.

"What are these for?" I asked her.

"I'm going to teach you embroidery," she said.

At that time children didn't argue and, anyway, the colours fascinated me. Eagerly I watched mother's needle.

But when I made a start it wasn't as easy as it looked. Mother could do neat, regular stitches, but I couldn't. My stitches looked like cats' teeth and I soon lost heart.

"I can't get it right," I moaned; I was an impatient child.

"There's no such word as can't - you have to keep trying," mother said gently. "You'll never do anything if you don't have patience."

That morning she left most of her housework to sit with me. She taught me slowly, stitch by stitch. Every ten minutes she went off to do some quick job, but she was back soon, encouraging me.

When at last I had done a whole daisy by myself she said, "There you are. You can do it if you try". Tears turned to smiles.

I kept on trying and began to make real progress.

When my favourite aunt came to tea mother said, "Go and get

your embroidery - show Auntie Sis what you've been doing."

I did as I was told, but a little reluctantly, because I knew that the best of grown-ups were critical. So I was quite unprepared for my aunt's reaction. "It's lovely. Will you make one for me?"

Surprised and pleased I agreed.

With mother's help to rely on I began to take my hobby quite seriously. As I stitched I listened to Children's Hour, living in the world of Romany and Toytown. When I'd made several tray cloths for Christmas presents, mother taught me how to cut out doll's clothes. "Just keep trying," she would say.

After Easter the doctor said I could go back to school. I was really rather scared because I'd been away so long. When mother took me to see the headmistress I was told I'd have to do extra homeword to help me catch up with the rest of the class.

Impossible? Difficult, certainly, but now I had acquired a secret store of confidence for I could embroider and I could make doll's clothes. Nobody else could do these things. My hope lay in trying - the magic word. At the end of term I passed the exams.

My schooling finished abruptly some years later when the war came and a bomb hit the school. I was just 14 so mother sent me to a secretarial college - about the only one in Liverpool left standing.

At first shorthand wasn't easy. But I knew that if you tried you could get results. And I did. Soon I was out of college working in a shipping office.

The hobby I learned as a child has been useful all my life. When I joined the WAAF it was useful on 'domestic night' and later, when

I married into the RAF it helped me pass many an hour on isolated RAF stations. It sparked off many conversations and helped me make many friends.

Recently, at the age of 62, I joined a tailoring class and today I make most of my clothes.

My wonderful mother didn't just teach me embroidery. She taught me the value of perseverance and the grace of patience.

May McCulloch, Folkestone

G K CHESTERTON is reported as saying,
"My country, right or wrong, is a thing that no patriot would think of saying except in a desperate case. It is like saying 'My mother, drunk or sober.'"

A LOVING NATURE

'Mother had to carry the drinking water three quarters of a mile'

MY MOTHER had a very hard childhood. She was the eldest of 14 children, two of whom were younger than me. I was born in Wales in 1927, the middle of three with a sister three years older and another sister four years younger.

In the cottage where we lived there was no running water. Mother had to carry all the drinking water three quarters of a mile. (My father worked nights - six nights a week - so we never saw much of him.)

All cooking was done on the living room fire and the only lighting was from oil lamps.

But in spite of these hardships we were the best loved and best dressed children. We were also the best fed, although how my mother did it I will never know as my father, although a regular worker, was low payed.

When we moved to Kent things became better but my mother still worked hard having bought a boarding house at the end of the war.

She has a wonderful loving nature and always said that my sisters and I meant the same to her, and she always treated us fairly. I think this helped make the three of us and and our children and grandchildren very good friends.

She is now in a nursing home and doesn't always know us, but I shall never forget when I went to visit her and she tried to stand up and hold her arms out to me, there was so much love in her eyes. We just held each other.

Barbara Cook, Ramsgate

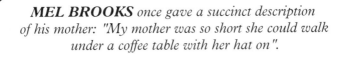

MEL BROOKS once gave a succinct description of his mother: "My mother was so short she could walk under a coffee table with her hat on".

90

MUM, AT WAR

'She could do almost anything when she put her mind to it'

S HE WAS Lil to my father, Auntie Lil to my cousin Alfie, and Mrs Wells to most of the neighbours. To us she was just mum, plain and simple, always around when we needed her.

Mum was about 32 when the Second World War began, although by today's standards she looked ten years older.

She was quite slim and only five feet three with small feet and hands. Her hair was dark brown although for most of the war years it was hidden from view by a headscarf. She wore this scarf up in a turban style with a knot at the front.

She did, once, make an effort to bring a bit of glamour into our mundane lives. She tied a strip of old stocking around her hair, then tucked up the hair into a kind of sausage roll around her head. It was different, but not easy to maintain what with dashing us children in and out of the air-raid shelter morning, noon and night.

This hairstyle was the source of dad's jokes, so she soon reverted back to the old headscarf, tied up munitions worker style.

She always wore over her dress, or skirt and blouse, the housewife's favourite of the time, a sleeveless floral wrap-over overall.

Her thin legs were clad in thick lisle stockings held up with garters. In winter these were topped with ankle socks. Mum always suffered with a red nose and dry, chapped hands, all due to poor diet and bad circulation no doubt.

The rough chapped hands were made worse by a job in a local cafe as a part-time washer-up.

My brother was always her favourite out of the two of us, probably because he almost died at birth. However, she never made any distinction between us as children be it with toys, sweet rations or clothes.

What a difficult time for any mother to clothe and feed a family during those war years.

I don't recall ever feeling hungry at all, I'm sure I never was.

My father would look at mum bustling around us as he, my brother and I sat at the meal table. "Where's yours then, Lil? Aren't you eating?"

Her reply was often, "Oh, I've already had mine," or, "I'll eat mine later when you lot have finished".

I think she ate the scraps which we left, if any, and probably gave us much of the rations which were due to her.

By the time I started my junior school, things on the home front had started to improve and morale with our soldiers

Mum makes me a dress for a music and elocution day. Auntie Ethel looks on

was high after their earlier battle defeats. Now peace was close at hand, just two years away from VE Day.

Our teachers at school were trying hard to bring some form of culture back into our young lives.

My mum was asked by our music teacher if I could go along with some other chosen applicants from our school and represent them at a music and elocution day to be held at the Baths Hall in Wimbledon.

Could mum find enough spare money to take me there? She could see my enthusiasm so said she would take time off from washing-up in the cafe to take me along.

The big day drew near and I asked for a new dress.

"My duck, I would give you the top brick off the chimney if I could, but you see there is no spare money and not enough clothing coupons."

I didn't care for her joke about chimneys. She could not palm me off like that. I wanted to look pretty, like that Shirley Temple kid on the pictures.

My Auntie Ethel offered a velvet bolero jacket encrusted in sequins which she had been given years before.

Mum declined saying it was far too nice to cut up.

I breathed a sigh of relief. If I'd gone up on the stage in that the audience would have expected me to wear a dirndl skirt, gipsey earrings and be able to play a violin.

Help eventually came to hand in the form of a kindly neighbour named Mrs Street.

She rummaged in her wardrobe and came out clutching a bundle of cloth. "How about that then! Old gold satin, will it do? It was the lining of a velvet evening cape, I don't think Harry and I will be doing much dancing now."

Mum's mouth was open and I was speechless.

In the shelter later that night, Mum was full of plans for that material. Over many nights she cut, and hand sewed. She even found five white buttons with my initial on them to fasten the front from neck to waist.

There was not enough material for a belt and a collar was too difficult for mum to shape.

The scissors had been borrowed from our neighbour because our own were always blunt.

Auntie Ethel was at hand for the moment of the 'big' fitting. I climbed up on to the kitchen table.

"Come on, Ethel," said my proud mum, "I've only got the hem to turn up now".

Auntie's eyes widened and she gave a sort of gasp. "My, you have been busy, Lil."

"Yes, it was a bit of a near miss, not much to play with," was mum's reply.

How true. I caught a glimpse of myself in the big mirror which hung over our fireplace. What did I look like? Definitely there was not the slightest resemblance between myself and Shirley Temple.

Auntie dug down into her shopping bag, and held up a brown velvet ribbon for my hair. It had come off a chocolate box years ago.

That was it! That's what I looked like as I walked out onto that stage with my headmistress and some of the school and other mothers looking on. Gold tight-fitting dress with my navy blue knickers just out of sight, knee-length fawn school socks and black laced-up shoes.

The tension around my chest and arms probably contributed to my nervous state. I did not get a bronze medal for my singing or poetry, only a certifcate.

Mum never knew just how disappointed I had been with that dress, although she must have had some idea as it was never worn again.

What a supreme effort by my dear mother to achieve all that for me! When it came to helping others, especially her children, nothing was too much trouble for her.

She did it all with infinite patience and unbounded love, which is why she was special to us.

You cannot ask any more than that from a mother.

Doreen Conroy, Surbiton

Happy memories to all Yours readers!

THE WAY YOU WERE

Treat yourself or a friend to a trip down memory lane with this delightful book of true-life tales from days gone by.

Written entirely by readers, The Way You Were is a nostalgic 100-page book with stories that will bring back many memories.

It costs £4.49 (p&p included). Please send a cheque or postal order made payable to YOURS Reader Offers, to:

The Way You Were,
YOURS Reader Offers,
PO Box 130,
Terrington St Clement,
Kings Lynn, Norfolk,
PE34 4RH.

Extra copies of My Marvellous Mum are also available, priced at £4.49 (p&p included), from the above address.

Compiled by the YOURS magazine team
Design by Sharon Palmer and David Reid.
Cover photograph by Tim Sandall